About the Author

Que Roland is a Native Detroiter that attended schools in Detroit while growing up, and even obtained Bachelors and Masters Degrees in Detroit. Que loves people and spending time with her 3 sons. Que loves flowers, interior design, reading, traveling, writing and embarking on new adventures.

Acknowledgements

I would like to thank all my family and friends who continue to inspire me to be great. I want to thank my boys for making me realize my greatness and continuing to teach me. I love you incessantly, you motivate me more than I could have ever imagined. I would like to thank ALL the men who I had the pleasure of learning from, and helped me navigate to the understanding of what love is and should be.

Reality Check Book

Lies

If a man tells you he has a woman/wife/significant other and you accept being in the 2nd, 3rd, or wherever you may fall, *please* keep in mind you will never have the #1 spot. Don't ever convince yourself that if he leaves his #1 that you will get that spot, he views you beneath a #1, he will get a new #1 before he ever considers you.

Reality Check No. 2

Flattery

If a man cheats with you, don't ever try to convince yourself that he prefers you! Don't flatter yourself ladies! That man is dishonest and untrustworthy and downright GREEDY.

Excuses

If a man bashes the woman he is in a relationship with when you meet him and he is using excuses of what his woman lacks as a reason he has a wandering eye and finds you appealing, run and hide they are all lies, lies, lies. Keep in mind ladies, if it were that bad, he would leave and make a life with you, no matter the reasons.

The Kids

If a man says "I'm with her because of my kids"! This is a piss poor excuse for his need for greed. Let's spin the perspective, yes he is telling the truth, he is staying for the kids. This situation has already been predetermined to be the best choice for his life. *"Home is where the heart is".*

Reality Check No. 5

Dating

If a man does not date you i.e.: dinner, movies, walks in the park, whatever tickles your fancy but makes frequent visits to YOUR home, STOP! THINK! MOVE ON! If this man cannot take you anywhere in or near a city that you or he resides, let's be real, he cannot risk being seen with you, this will never flourish into a legitimate relationship.

Reality Check No. 6

Careless

If a man has gotten so careless to allow his "sidechick" to get your personal information to contact you. Read this carefully, **Never** and I mean **never** indulge in the secrets and lies she has to offer about your man.! 9 out of 10 her intentions are not to help you but rather hurt. You know YOUR man, kindly end that call and check his ass, never ever let her see you sweat!

Reality Check No. 7

The Family

If a man never introduces you to his female family members, but flaunts you proudly around his guy family and friends, *please and I beg* you not to overlook this detail. Ladies, meeting and getting to know ALL of his family is VERY important. Most female family members cannot hide a cheating man's secrets even if they are family and will not be comfortable with the lies especially if she has a relationship with that man's full time lover.

(Y'all know what I'm talking about)

Reality Check No. 8

Secrets

If a man never allows you to come to his home, STOP, HAUL ASS! Wait this should be *Reality Check No. 1*

Reality Check No. 9

Broke

If a man asks you to borrow money within the 1st year of dating, no matter the reason, this would be a good reason to pause and ask yourself if you should answer his calls anymore. A man should never ask a woman for money... (just my opinion)

Mama's Boy

If a man appears to have an Oedipus complex with his mother (**behaves likes he wants to be in a relationship with his mother**), true we all want a man whom adores his mom but this can become problematic if there aren't clear boundaries defined within this triangular relationship. Set limits and stick to them.

Reality Check No. 11

The Chase

If a man is not chasing you, Don't you dare think about chasing him...Dating 101, seems really simple huh. Since little girls we have been told that a man should love you more than you love them, ladies this may not be such a cliché, allow a man to be a man and pursue you and properly court you. Don't forget you deserve it.

Control

If a man hates ALL your friends, don't try to figure this one out, he isn't the right man for you. The man is probably controlling and insecure and we all need our friends from time to time and should be allowed to keep them without guilt or permission. Most men who hate ALL your friends don't want you to have any. Please do not confuse this with him wanting more of your attention.

Reality Check No. 13

Insecure

If a man finds ways to make you feel insecure about who you are and you never had these issues previously, now all of sudden you almost think you are crazy at times...rethink this relationship, no loving man would make his woman feel bad about herself, especially intentionally.

Reality Check No. 14

You're Awesome

If you find yourself losing your awesomeness, keep your head and attitude together. Don't ever let your man forget your specialness, keep him on his toes, keep your appearance impeccable, keep your goals intact, keep getting your own money, and make all those around you stop and stare, including him.

Reality Check No. 15

Forgiveness

If your man has a child outside of your relationship and you decide to stay and forgive. Allow this man to have a relationship with his child. A real man takes care of his children, however they arrived in the world.

Reality Check No. 16

Peace

If your man says he needs space, give it to him, you may find peace in getting to know yourself by having some alone time. If you think being with your man 24/7 will prevent him from straying, you are dead wrong, "when there is a will, there is a way".

Reality Check No. 17

B*TCH

If your man seems to forget who you are, (ie: not noticing how special you are and what he has in you) always demand that he treats you like a ***fucking lady.***

Reality Check No. 18

Yummy

If your man wants dirty sex, don't be afraid to try new things as long as your integrity is not in question and you trust him. Have Plenty of Fun with this one!

Reality Check No. 19

Goodbye

If your man is a repeat offender in the game of cheating, and you decide you have had enough. The greatest payback is simply walking away QUIETLY; this means NO drama. It will kill him eternally.

Reality Check No. 20

Pretty

In conclusion, stay honest with yourself, respect your relationship, and fight fairly, allow each other to speak, remain calm, sometimes it's best to walk away and revisit but don't ever leave issues unresolved and allow them to boil over. Always remember, pretty is, is what pretty does. Ladies our spirit is strong and powerful and heard without even speaking…Stay Pretty!!!